In the beginning, God created the vastness of the heavens and the richness of the earth. And in His act of creation, He crafted a myriad of animals, each according to its kind. Thus, He gave life to beings that swim, fly, and roam the earth (Genesis 1:20-25). Each creature, a unique reflection of the divine craft, was set forth to thrive and unravel the beauty of creation. God saw that it was good, and graced the earth with the splendor of living diversity.

Jocélio Louzeiro

2023

This Book Belongs to:

Test Color Page